Paul –

Hope you enjoy.

Matt

LEADING

<u>WITH</u> COURAGE

Daily Reminders for the Decision Maker

BY MATTHEW WHITE
AND JUDITH BELL

WESTBOW
PRESS®
A DIVISION OF THOMAS NELSON
& ZONDERVAN

WestBow Press books may be ordered through booksellers or by contacting:

WestBow Press
A Division of Thomas Nelson & Zondervan
1663 Liberty Drive
Bloomington, IN 47403
www.westbowpress.com
1 (866) 928-1240

ISBN: 978-1-5127-1623-8 (hc)
ISBN: 978-1-5127-1621-4 (e)

Library of Congress Control Number: 2015916800

Bookmasters, Ashland Ohio

WestBow Press rev. date: 1/22/2016

DEDICATION

I dedicate this book to my employees, mentors, clients, and customers—to those who have taught me so much of what is written here.

Acknowledgments

Thank you to Judith Bell, the world's best coach. Thank you for reading, editing, and adding to my original draft, helping me to bring structure to my flood of thoughts.

Thanks also to Mike Rossman, my college roommate and amazing friend. Thank you for seeing that this book was completed.

Lastly, a special thank you to my amazing wife, Melissa, and our two wonderful children Emily and Zachary. You have tolerated me through so much with unconditional love.

CONTENTS

INTRODUCTION   xi

PART 1: TAKE CARE OF YOURSELF

1 • Live a Balanced Life   1

2 • Trust Yourself   9

3 • Develop Yourself   15

4 • Be a Leader   29

5 • Value Innovation   39

6 • Beware Self-Deception   51

7 • Embrace Ethics   57

8 • Learn From Failure   63

9 • Pay It Forward   69

10 • Lead Your Family Business Well   77

PART 2: THEN BUILD A GREAT TEAM

11 • Be Confident   85

12 • Learn to Listen   99

13 • Create a Learning Environment   113

14 • Develop Your Employees   123

15 • Cultivate a Positive Attitude   131

16 • Become a Great Team Leader   145

17 • Practice Good Decision Making   165

18 • Lead Through Choices and Accountability   173

19 • Create Partners, Customers, and Vendors For Life   185

FINAL REMINDER   191

INTRODUCTION

I clearly remember the brief calm that surrounded my life and family during the summer of 2005. It was a passing moment, but it illuminated my unrelenting drive to succeed. It also provided a glimpse into my future, revealing several important and challenging decisions I needed to make. That summer, at the age of 36, I completed the largest transaction in the history of a family business my parents had started thirty-one years before. To both celebrate and unwind from the rigors of closing the deal, my family and I travelled to Nantucket Island for a vacation that included reconnecting with old college friends. Privately, I hoped to reclaim the part of me that could experience joy. I wanted once again to join in and laugh with family and friends. This included finding the humility to even laugh at myself.

However, this trip was different from past vacations that we had scheduled to reward ourselves for the sacrifices involved in building the company. To me, it seemed this lucrative deal should have embodied all I had worked for. Certainly, it had resulted in a highly profitable transaction that provided financial security for my family, along with strong returns for trusting investors.

But instead of being able to relax and bask in my victory, I found myself confronted with an unrelenting need to consider a new perspective—a new approach to how I lived my life. Though I did not yet realize it, at that time, I lived in a funnel of organized chaos. The vacation I had looked forward to—the temporary disruption in my fast-paced life—only caused me to question my lifestyle. Frustration followed, triggered by my reluctant acknowledgment that what I had expected to be a life-changing business transaction wasn't going to satisfy me. "If this isn't enough, what is?" I asked myself. I didn't have an answer.

Around the same time, I began to notice an increasing number of news reports of a wide range of white-collar crimes. This combination of how I felt and what I was reading caused me to consider what was right and wrong with American business and the culture created around it. I continued to reflect on my own life and how in my 20s and early 30s I had wanted to conquer the business world—a dream driven by my growing ego. I wanted notoriety, money, and fame. The adrenalin of it all was addicting.

Looking back, I can now see the signs of emotional stress leading up to my company's landmark deal. My fuse grew shorter as I became more successful. Because of my increased moodiness, my wife and kids avoided me. I understood, but remained silent. By the end of the average work week, they wanted very little to do with me. Over the weekend, in an attempt to get in their good graces by Sunday night, I would pretend I was not consumed by work. Then on Monday, the cycle would start over. This routine had become a normal part of my life at home; I simply chose to ignore what my life was becoming.

There were also physical effects. Five years prior, in my early 30s, I was forced into the initial stages of thinking more deeply about life and how much control I really had. At 31, I was diagnosed with type 1 diabetes. It did not make sense—the diagnosis of childhood diabetes in a 31-year-old man with no family history of diabetes. Until that moment, I had believed myself invincible. Yet I determined that even diabetes could not stop me, and I faced it like I had every other obstacle in my life. Learning all I could, I attempted to control the disease with insulin, a better diet, and more exercise.

Surely, I thought, through hard work I could manage the disease with the same success that I had managed my business. However, despite all my efforts, I experienced only moderate improvement, and to me, moderation was failure. Because blood sugar levels don't lie, I was left with one option—accept the real reason for my health deterioration. There was little doubt; the stress associated with how I lived my professional life was already taking its toll.

Because I had bought into the lie that led to my need to be in complete control, I pushed the limits of my body and mind. I refused to stop until I reached the finish line and was victorious, never allowing myself to focus on anything other than the "goal." The "prize." The problem was, I always started another deal, entered another race, before the current one was finished. The constant pressure allowed me to avoid the truth that the "goal" was unfulfilling.

When I closed the 2005 business transaction, I capitalized on the opportunity to sell what amounted to 70 percent of our business—a deal that took more than a year to complete. It was a huge win for our investors and my family. During the year of negotiations, I dreamed about how life would improve afterward. I would be wealthy, flush with cash, and free to do all the things I love to do but had not had time for. To me, it was the be all and end all.

But the day after the deal closed and funds were disbursed, I awoke with the emptiest feeling in my life. *What did I do? Why did I do it?* I wondered. What I had done was put a price tag on something I was passionate about and sold a part of my life that gave me great purpose. I did this because I thought the resulting wealth would bring freedom and allow me to sustain the elusive peace I had sporadically experienced throughout my career. At that moment, I realized I had been focusing my entire life on the end result, the goal—not the process of getting there. Suddenly I saw that everything I thought I knew about living my life was backwards. This was my first true moment of clarity.

Since then, I've realized life is a journey on which most of us are searching for a path to greater happiness. Becoming conscious about the decisions in our lives is the first step toward creating greater happiness. Unfortunately, many of us, like me, spend years on a path that takes us farther and farther away from what really makes us happy. Ironically, it is our ego that trips us up. Fueled by our insecurities, our ego talks to us, telling us we need to achieve more, make more money, and win at all costs. This inner voice creates more stress and pressure, causing us to spend less time with our families. We invest little of our most valuable asset—time—to gain a better understanding of the future impact of the decisions we make today. This includes areas outside of business. Such a lifestyle can quickly become a never-ending prison where we live a life that does not bring us true fulfillment and happiness. This was the story of my life until I realized I was doing it all wrong.

In response, I began writing this book as a reminder to myself, first of all, about what is important in my life. Through the process, I now realize the authentic experience of being present—accompanied by a heightened awareness of gratitude for the journey I am on—does not require effort and sacrifice. However, the conscious decision to pause and take a deep breath, which leads to it, does. In fact, it can be an outright battle. To this day, I struggle with consciousness and living in the present. I am still learning how to make the truths found here a reality in my life. Yet, when I revisit my documented experiences, I find permission to shut down the dominant part of my brain that resists. For that reason, I read them often.

I believe we all can benefit from regular reminders of the principles of leadership and success in life and business contained in this book. I hope this book will serve as a reminder and guide for you just as it has for me. To that end, I invite you to join me on this journey of discovery. May we all find true fulfillment.

PART 1

take care of yourself

All the wealth in the world has brought little happiness and cannot buy good health. Even if you are the most successful person, your greatest success should be that you know who you are and what the real priorities are.

—*Lou Giraudo*

1 • LIVE A BALANCED LIFE

Live a balanced life where the importance of heart, health, and mind align with work, socializing, family, and fun. Balance creates peace, clarity, restoration, and motivation.

Know your priorities. Understand the difference between what you can do and what you should do.

If you want to have a family, your
family must come first.

Maintaining balance in your life is critical to your personal health and to your company's long-term health. You are deceiving yourself if you believe you don't have time for balance. Take care of yourself, as well as your family and friends. You will all notice and appreciate the difference.

Create short rituals that are replenishing—such as a walk, meditation, exercise, or even a nap. Innovation and creative problem solving are best done when you are in a relaxed, non-stressed state.

Operating a successful business means managing a fluid and constantly changing organism in which the deadwood of obsolete ideas needs to be thrown away and new ideas must be generated. This means a leader should never be satisfied and should consistently look for new and better ways to keep progressing. Although this may make it hard to relax and live a balanced life, a balanced life is also critical to a good leader and must be cultivated with equal enthusiasm.

2 • TRUST YOURSELF

A formal education in business does not take the place of experience and common sense. Develop trust in yourself by reflecting on each success and each failure, determining what is valuable and using the lessons to inform your future.

When you are deciding between an option based on business theory and an option based on your gut, go with your gut. If you learn to discern what your gut is telling you, it will become your best decision-making tool.

At times, the public, markets, stockholders, employees, and even your family may think you are nuts. Listen to them and weigh their opinions. However, if you believe your course is logical, have the confidence and courage to stay the course despite what they say.

Skepticism in the right areas at the right time is critical. Skepticism in the wrong areas at the wrong time is fatal. It is important to know when to be skeptical.

3 • DEVELOP YOURSELF

Always have a mentor. Your mentor will change through your life as you seek balance, achieve goals, learn, and grow. First and foremost, your mentor should have a moral and ethical standard you respect. Second, your mentor must have made career decisions that you will be facing. However, your mentor does not need to be in the same business as you for you to receive value.

Always remember that you are extremely important to the people in your company. They look up to you and watch your every move. Be conscious of your actions, words, and attitudes, remembering their potential for impact.

Successful leaders know their job is half counselor and coach and half business strategist and visionary. At different points, one will be more important than the other. You don't have to become a counselor, but you do have to understand people. The place to start is with yourself. The best leaders continually develop greater self-awareness.

Study people. Learn what motivates them and is important to them. Find out why people get triggered and defensive. You need to understand each person who reports directly to you better than they understand themselves.

Leaders are responsible to adapt their management style to fit the personalities of each directly-reporting employee. If you want to get the most out of your team, learn to be flexible in order to bring out the best in people with different personalities and temperaments.

Hire people who are smarter or better than you at what they do. If you are the smartest and the most capable person in the company, it will never be any better than you. That will only take you so far. Your team should be much greater than any individual member, including you. But you will only create this kind of dynamic team when you no longer feel threatened by the successes of others.

Work on yourself: Courageously face yourself without self-deception in order to become increasingly self-aware; look at yourself with compassion and understanding rather than self-recrimination; and take positive action based on your insights.

Forget the John Wayne school of management. No one gets as far alone as they do with others. No athlete reaches the pinnacle of success without training and coaching. Learning about business is not the same as learning about yourself. Find a consultant or coach, and make a commitment to your own development.

Developing business acumen requires practice
and time. So does learning about yourself.
Be patient, relentless, and self-forgiving.

Separate your personal happiness from your business. If your self-identity and your feelings of self-worth and happiness come from your business, you will put pressure on your employees to be perfect. No one is perfect. Work on yourself until you feel happy with yourself, regardless of your role and responsibilities.

Feedback is the most readily available, but often the least used, source of learning. Consider getting feedback from people at every level of your organization on a regular basis— including your customers and vendors.

Feedback allows you to self-correct before the market does it for you. Develop your self-esteem so you will welcome feedback rather than fear it.

Read books, listen to audio teachings, and attend seminars. Keep widening and deepening your own knowledge base. Commit to being a life-long learner. As John F. Kennedy said, "Leadership and learning are indispensable to each other."

4 • BE A LEADER

You are lucky to be the CEO;

treat it that way.

The CEO's priorities should be as follows:

1. Moral and ethical conscience
2. Employees
3. Customers
4. Shareholders

If you do a good job with 1–3, 4 will take care of itself.

The CEO is not the most important person in an organization. The people who execute the CEO's vision are the most important.

Set the vision, create the goals to achieve the vision, and help your team do what's needed to meet the goals. Then follow a strict discipline focused on vision, goals, and strategies.

Your employees want to know you have vision and you understand how they are included in that vision. They want to know that you have the required passion, determination, and strength to lead and that you value their personal and professional qualities and how those qualities will help achieve the strategies and goals.

Your vision is more likely to succeed when your team buys into the vision and makes it their own. Take time to communicate and show them the wisdom behind your vision.

The day you decide you have beaten the competition is the day your business loses its competitive edge. Your job as the leader is to evolve the vision. That motivates people and keeps them from resting on their laurels.

Remember this old Japanese saying: Vision without action is a dream. Action without vision is a nightmare.

5 • VALUE INNOVATION

To be a good leader, you must be both smart and willing to take chances. America will only keep its competitive edge if we have the courage to risk.

Improvement is always possible. If you are openly enthusiastic about innovation, your employees will be more likely to embrace and initiate change.

Innovation is vital, and change is necessary. You must not allow yourself to fall in love with any aspect of your business. Everything must be able to be challenged. At the simplest level, business is a group of people always trying to do something better. Develop a group that functions as a closely knit team, and they will produce a better product, guaranteed.

Discourage the philosophy, "That's how we do it here." It will only cause stagnation. Help your employees navigate change gracefully by developing their capacities and competencies. People and businesses that are most adaptive to change will be most likely to survive.

To maintain market share and stay ahead of the competition, you must embrace innovation. Empower your team to innovate, and remove artificial and unnecessary levels of hierarchy. Create only the necessary structure in a way that functions smoothly and efficiently.

Constantly strive to eliminate bureaucracy.

As you grow, this becomes more important.

Without constant attention to streamlining,

you will become sluggish, making you a perfect

target for more agile competitors to crush.

Sometimes there is no room in a market for a good company, but there is always room for a great company.

When looking for innovative solutions in any part of your business, first define the problem broadly without suggesting how to solve it. If you define the limits of a box (solution) narrowly, people will struggle to step out of the box and think creatively.

Wonder about everything.

6 • BEWARE SELF-DECEPTION

You can't be truthful with others until you are truthful with yourself. Don't confuse what you want something to be with what it is. Self-deception is a mistake many small business owners and leaders make. It takes courage to recognize what is.

Look at your company's actual performance data realistically and face problems directly. Doing otherwise is a slippery slope.

Being a leader can be incredibly lonely. At times, you may need to vent. Find a coach, consultant, friend, spouse, or peer who can listen to you without feeling burdened. Ask permission before you vent. However, never vent to your employees, regardless of how much you trust them.

7 • Embrace Ethics

Conscious leaders have high ethical and moral standards. If your ethics guide your interactions with your employees and your customers, your company will prosper and your shareholders will be happy.

The idea of corporate fraud is a myth; all fraud is caused by individuals and is, therefore, personal.

Likewise, corporate greed is also a
myth; all greed is personal.

A big difference exists between what is morally and ethically correct and what is legally correct. If you first review an idea through a moral and ethical lens, you will have little need to explore its legality.

8 · LEARN FROM FAILURE

It is okay to fail as long as you have given it your all and are operating with the highest ethical standards. Failure is a part of business and life. If you left no stone unturned in your pursuit of success and maintained high ethical standards, you can accept your failure and transform it into a learning opportunity.

The world is run by leaders who know how
to fail, pick themselves up, and start again.
Celebrate yourself for taking a chance at success,
reflect on what went wrong, and move on.

Bad times are often the fertilizer for good times. Business is cyclical, and someone or something will always try to defeat your product. Rewards come when you make a better deal on the heels of a loss. If you use defeat to motivate you even more to succeed, that success will be even sweeter.

No one understands the aerodynamics of flying by contemplating how things stay on the ground. When a plan fails, take the time to discover why it was unsuccessful; then correct the mistake and move forward.

9 • PAY IT FORWARD

Be humble. You are lucky to have what you have and to be where you are. You are not inherently special or better than others. No matter how you came to be in the position you now occupy, consider that your position is a privilege, and with it comes the responsibility to pass on the gifts of time, money, caring, and love.

Many people in your life have positively impacted your career. Make sure you intentionally support the next generation of leaders.

Philanthropy is the most selfish thing

you can do, and that's okay.

Serve your community. You owe it to them.

If you have the financial resources, invest in new companies to keep innovation moving forward.

10 · LEAD YOUR FAMILY BUSINESS WELL

The key to a family business is empathy. The parents must understand the children's drive to innovate and make the business their own, and the children must understand the parents' complex and often conflicted feelings about leaving the business.

During each stage of employment, the parents must balance training the children with leaving them enough latitude to experiment and grow. Similarly, before beginning to innovate, the children must appreciate their parents' contribution to the success of the company and learn the strategies, practices, and procedures that made the company successful.

Family businesses require a high degree of emotional intelligence. Because of the complexity of family business relationships, even with a great deal of consciousness, they are often very stressful. Don't assume you know how to communicate and make decisions well just because you are family. Ensure the success of your company by investing in the transition and the ongoing interpersonal dynamics of the family members. Just as you draw on legal resources when faced with legal matters, draw on resources that will help you navigate succession planning, decision making, conflict resolution, and relationship building.

Don't take your family members for granted. Many people treat their family members worse than they would ever treat a friend or employee. They make assumptions, take offense, and jump to conclusions far more easily with relatives than with others. Because of this tendency, create a structure that helps family members clear up potential misunderstandings before they blow up.

PART 2

build a great team

Caring to know and understand what
motivates people is one of the most critical
skills to have.

—John Jack

11 • BE CONFIDENT

Confidence is critical; arrogance is fatal. Confidence develops from the inside out. When you truly feel competent, you exude confidence. By contrast, arrogance stems from unacknowledged and often unconscious insecurities or fears about yourself. It is an attempt to cover up your insecurities. Authentic confidence develops from the courage to face your own insecurities.

Most business indecisions are the result of insecurities in leaders. Insecure leaders need to be liked, perceived as competent, and seen as important. These needs often cause indecisiveness, impulsiveness, aggression, rationalization, and short-sightedness.

Many leaders try to hide their insecurities and don't seek help. However, great leaders are aware of their frailties, understand their limitations, and seek support.

Passion is critical to your success. It inspires you and gives you the stamina to overcome obstacles. However, don't confuse passion with defensiveness. Learn to recognize the difference.

If you want to create a highly productive work environment, as the leader, you must model open and accountable communication. When you express your feelings and show your vulnerability, you give your employees permission to do the same. This will create greater trust and lead to much better communication and teamwork.

We are all vulnerable. If you try to avoid vulnerability, you will become defensive. If you are defensive, then your team will be defensive. You will not be able to deliver constructive feedback and your employees will not be able to receive it. Little that is positive can be accomplished in a defensive environment.

Set an example by exposing your vulnerability. Let your employees see you admit a mistake, a fear, an apology. That will do more to create a learning environment than anything else.

Don't be a victim, a bully, a rescuer, or a martyr.
Each role becomes a self-fulfilling prophecy.
Learn to recognize your defensive behaviors
and attitudes and change them so you can
lead authentically rather than defensively.

Use email to communicate information
but not to address interpersonal issues.

When you read an email, remember that you are reading words without voice tone and facial expressions. Avoid interpreting the other person's words or making assumptions about that person's intentions. Give your teammates the benefit of the doubt. Better yet, ask questions with an attitude of curiosity and inquiry. Most people respond well to open, non-judgmental questions and poorly to accusations.

You know you're being defensive when you take things personally, when your reaction is pervasive (it shows up in many areas of your life), and you experience this reaction or a similar one frequently. Instead of blaming and shaming yourself for reacting defensively, learn how to use a positive inner voice to calm down and bring a different perspective to the situation.

12 • LEARN TO LISTEN

Good communication (and leadership) is 90 percent listening and 10 percent talking. The most common mistake made in any relationship—business or personal—is talking too much and listening too little. Highly effective people will seek first to understand and then to be understood.

The most important question in business is why? Ask why—not in accusation, but in curiosity and genuine interest. You know you have found the right business when your internal passion for understanding won't let you stop asking why? Ask because you are genuinely curious and are looking for a better way. If you don't care enough to ask why, find a new business.

Spread the **why** philosophy throughout your culture so that those who report to you have the courage to question you and each other without fear of defensive reactions or retribution.

The quality of people's responses is based on the quality of your questions. Learn how to ask open-ended questions—starting with *how, what,* and *why*—and you'll receive higher quality and more thorough information than if you ask yes-or-no questions.

Find your true curiosity before you ask a question. People will perceive any judgment you may feel in your voice or face. If you cultivate curiosity, you'll create a learning environment where employees take appropriate risks, ask good questions, and are more innovative.

Behind every successful leader is an understanding
and supportive spouse or family. Trust me—
you can be very difficult to live with.

Keep an open mind. Suspend judgment about people and their ideas until you've taken the time to understand them.

Listening seems easy until you're triggered and reactive. Then it's difficult to stop a kneejerk reaction that sounds like, "No, you're wrong. You don't know what you're talking about." Difficult as it is, calming down to avoid reacting is more than worth it. Your employees will not feel heard if you react defensively, even if that reaction is silent. Authentic listening happens when you calm down and respond with genuine curiosity.

A genuinely curious listener is a rare gift. Give the gift of listening deeply frequently.

The more we know what we don't
know, the more we will know.

Empathy has been undervalued in the business world.
If you develop your ability to listen empathically,
your workforce will go the extra mile for you.

Empathy lets people know that you're listening and you understand. It doesn't necessarily mean you agree or perceive the situation similarly. It just means you're able to put yourself in their position long enough to understand why they feel or think as they do. Even if empathy is not your strong suit, choose to work at it. Your employees will feel valued and cared for when you take the time to listen empathically.

Every company needs a healthy system of checks and balances. When you create a learning environment where people are free to question, you ensure the viability of your product. In this environment, validating technical data, checking each other's reasoning, and balancing each other's hopes and expectations will become a vital part of team interactions and will keep your business on track with the changing marketplace.

When you stumble—and you will—family and satisfied employees will be there to pick you up. Create a learning environment where everyone benefits from the lessons learned through your risk-taking and mistakes. Consider defining mistakes as "opportunities to learn, redirect, and explore a new direction."

Certain kinds of conflict are healthy for an organization, because they provide a system of checks and balances and create fertile ground for innovation. Support passionate, well-intentioned conflict.

Your financial people will be more conservative than you. Expect that and welcome it. Use their concerns to motivate you to improve your due diligence, not to determine the course of your actions.

If you let the financial people make decisions about new business, you'll go out of business.

Leaders tend to be optimistic. They look toward what might be. Financial people tend to be pessimistic. They look toward the potential problems associated with the risk. Both perspectives are important to the organization and balance of one another.

Resist reprimanding people for making a wrong decision. Instead, seek to understand how they arrived at their conclusion. Celebrate wrong decisions made through a healthy critical analysis. Encourage people to continue making decisions.

14 • DEVELOP YOUR EMPLOYEES

Every business and individual has unlimited potential. Productive teams are composed of a series of relationships or pairs. Successful pairs are made up of individuals who are flexible, non-defensive, motivated, and skilled at communication and creative problem solving. The best investment you can make in your company is the development of each individual.

Empower those who report to you directly to make more and more decisions. The more they own their contributions to the business, the more they will want to make it succeed. If you teach them to pass this down through the ranks, you will have an unstoppable workforce.

Only accept excellence. Respond to anything less with a firm but loving hand. When you call forward the best in your employees, you will not only raise their performance, but you will also raise their self-esteem. High performance comes from people who feel good about themselves and their contributions. If you berate or shame your employees, you will create a climate of fear and mediocrity. No one has ever been shamed or criticized into excellence.

The employees who have direct contact with your

customers know the most about the customers.

These employees are also your best advertising.

Hire people who like people, develop them,

and use them as a resource to better understand,

retain, and develop new customers.

Many believe feelings interfere with efficient business. However, it is the inability to deal with our feelings that causes the problem. Because no one really leaves their feelings at the door, train your employees to process and express their feelings constructively. As your workforce becomes more skillful at addressing feelings openly, you will actually have less drama, less gossip, and greater productivity in your business.

15 • CULTIVATE A POSITIVE ATTITUDE

Find the positive in everything. It's there; just keep looking. This ability is important for both life and business.

Treat your customers and employees with respect. If you listen to their concerns and let them know you care, you'll greatly reduce the risk of losing them.

When faced with a difference of opinion, let
the other person win if it is not critical.

Not everything is critical. Don't sweat the
small stuff—and most of it is small stuff.

Allow your passion for your employees, your product, and your customers to motivate your leadership. Lead because you want to pass on your attitude that work can be pleasurable, rewarding, and even fun. Strive as a leader because you want the challenges that lead to the thrill of victory. Do not strive as a leader because you desire power, money, fame, or love. These motives originate in insecurity and will lead to eventual failure, unhappiness, or feelings of emptiness.

In business, if something happens quickly, it's for one of two reasons: because it's incorrect or poorly done or because you got lucky. Success takes time. Be patient.

Celebrate the small and the large
victories, but never rest on them.

Enjoy the societal position you've attained, but don't let it go to your head. Self-conscious and smug attitudes do not breed innovation. They breed mediocrity, causing you to become more concerned with what others think than with taking chances to achieve something great. Those who are truly successful are driven by a passion to be the best, not a desire to impress others.

Being good at something is easy. Being great takes work. Be great! It's worth it.

Never underestimate the power of your will.
The stronger your passion is for what you are
doing, the stronger your will to get it done.

At times, you may think all you have is your will. Use it when it will help you, but don't confuse it with power, and don't let it feed your ego. Don't use your will to steamroll others. Instead, let it feed your confidence as you learn to use your will to support everyone's success.

Business is a game. As in all games, there are winners and losers. Compete to win, but always treat your opponents respectfully.

16 • BECOME A GREAT TEAM LEADER

A leader's success is determined by the people who carry out his or her vision. If you appreciate the importance of each person's contribution, you will create a thriving culture and a successful business.

Show your employees your appreciation by compensating them fairly. Your long-term success depends on their success.

You are lucky to be a leader. Appreciate your good fortune and lead in a way that makes your employees feel valued, respected, and cared for. When you do, they will follow you energetically and enthusiastically. You can't put a price tag on that.

The best leaders are visionaries and innovators who have a high risk tolerance and a keen appreciation for the people who work for them. Intelligence, vision, and determination in a leader will never take the place of a motivated and satisfied workforce. Remember—people are your business. Treat your employees as you would your most valued customers.

Employees are more productive when they feel appreciated for their contributions, challenged by their work, and cared about by those above them. Compensation alone will not motivate people as effectively as appreciation, challenge, and compassion.

Criticism is important and necessary for excellence,
but make sure to do it constructively.

Most young MBAs know far less
than they think.

Find the positive in everything. You will find
it if you keep looking. A positive atmosphere
is intrinsic to a high-performance culture.

Do not allow generosity to be motivated by guilt. Those who receive such gifts usually sense the lack of authenticity. As a result, they will not feel appreciated, and they will not appreciate the gift. Develop your ability to appreciate and give credit to the many people who do their part to move projects forward to success.

Your employees will rarely understand or appreciate the stress and pressures you face as the leader. They may feel entitled to a larger share of the profits without recognizing the risks you may have taken. Be generous, in a desire to reward those who helped create the team's success, without giving away the store.

If you treat your employees as if they could be employees for life, you will create a loyal workforce.

As the leader, your job is to give the credit for your organization's success to the employees and to take the responsibility for the organization's failures. In doing so, you will build loyal employees who want to excel and innovate.

Have fun and laugh often.

People matter more than profit. If you pay attention to the bottom line without considering the people, you may have short term success, but you will not thrive in the long run. If you hire the right people and regularly invest in them, you will continue to create profit.

People flourish when they are appreciated and acknowledged for their contributions. If you want to build a motivated workforce, be authentic and generous with positive recognition.

Support your employees in their own time of personal struggle. And remember, at such times, they need a friend, not a boss. You will have employees who are dealing with death, addiction, divorce, and other difficult issues. Help them. Make efforts and use your resources to get them to a better place. At minimum, you did the right thing. At most, you built loyalty that will last forever.

Lead by example. Don't ask your employees
to do something you aren't willing to do.

17 • PRACTICE GOOD DECISION MAKING

Leadership has nothing to do with making
popular decisions. It has everything to
do with making hard decisions.

If you include your employees in decisions that affect them, they will invest their discretionary emotional energy in the company.

You will make better decisions when you make them with the long term in mind. We all know people who think in the short run. They are usually trying to get rich quick, and they are rarely successful. Success comes from attention, intention, and commitment.

A decision is not made until the team has determined what action step will occur, who will do it, what time frame the action will happen in, and how and when the information will be reported back to the team. Once these details have been written and agreed upon, then the decision is final.

A culture of accountability is based on
trust, which is developed when people
communicate openly and act responsibly.

18 • LEAD THROUGH CHOICES AND ACCOUNTABILITY

When dealing with the rules and regulations that govern all business, it is important to travel down two separate paths simultaneously. On the one hand, accept certain regulations as part of the obstacle course to victory. On the other hand, fight to change what is outdated, ineffective, or inefficient. Never, however, let bureaucracy be an excuse for failure.

No excuses. Period. No whining either.

We all have choices regarding our thoughts and actions. Choose to believe you can accomplish your goals and have a balanced life. Even if you don't believe it at first, adopt it as a practice as if it is true. You'll be surprised at how empowered you feel and at the level of consciousness you bring to your choices.

If you don't like your career path, change it.

Take responsibility for your own fulfillment.

Luck is not a good business model, unless your definition of luck is "opportunity plus preparedness," as it is for the Somali Bantu tribes.

There is no place in an organization for someone
who does not take responsibility for poor decisions.

Leadership and organizational practices that focus on self-preservation to avoid criticism and responsibility are like cancer to a company. Create a culture of accountability where it is safe to admit mistakes. Believe that you can create what you want in your business. Of course, good strategy and plans are crucial.

Set realistic expectations for your stockholders and meet them within five percent to the positive or negative. If you miss to the upside, it is still a surprise, and many people don't like surprises—even good ones.

Employees who don't fit in with your company culture will be more destructive than employees who don't fulfill their responsibilities acceptably. Develop the latter, but fire the former.

20 • CREATE PARTNERS, CUSTOMERS

AND VENDORS FOR LIFE

Your business will work better if your vendors and suppliers make money while doing business with you. They'll help you make more money if they thrive as a result of their relationship with you.

Think about how successful American business could be if we transferred the energy spent on fighting bureaucracy and used it on our customers. Accept the bureaucratic obstacles for what they are, and move your attention to what really matters—your customers.

If the customer is always right, structure your organization to focus on the customer, not the CEO. The CEO is usually farthest from the customer.

Make an effort with and embrace people who are closed-minded. The fact that most people won't do this will give you a major competitive advantage.

21 • FINAL REMINDER

Allow peace in your life. May God bless you with the strength to be a courageous leader, the wisdom to enjoy the journey, and the self-confidence to pursue and appreciate a balanced life.

About the Authors

Matt White is the chief executive officer of Basin Street Properties. As the chief executive, he is responsible for both developing and managing Basin Street's strategic direction and the direction of its investments. Under Matt's leadership, Basin Street has grown to encompass major investments throughout Northern California and Northern Nevada, including a broad range of Class-A office, mixed use, industrial, retail, apartment, and hotel properties.

Matt began his career in the family business twenty-one years ago as a project manager, handling the leasing and construction in Sonoma, Marin, and Napa Counties. He later became the chief financial officer. As CFO, among other duties, he established and managed the Basin Street Properties Investor Program, performing assessment and analysis for acquisitions and providing strategic real estate advice and support to investors.

In 2005, Matt negotiated Basin Street's largest transaction through the sale of 36 buildings, totaling 1.4 million square feet. In 2012, he then negotiated the re-acquisition of much of that portfolio at a greatly discounted price.

Matt has a BA in political science from Boston University. As one who is dedicated to his family and small mountain community, he currently sits on the Board of Trustees of Lake Tahoe School. Additionally, Matt enjoys supporting his two children's sports activities, including being the assistant coach for the high school varsity basketball team. In his free time, he is an avid cyclist and skier and enjoys the challenge of a good basketball game or mountain bike race.

Judith Bell, MS, is founder and president of Rewire Leadership Institute®. A master facilitator, consultant, teacher, and coach, she has created and facilitated personal growth, team development and organizational change seminars, coached executives and teams, facilitated strategic planning for high visibility meetings, and supported culture change for over four decades. She works with a diverse range of companies, from government agencies, non-profits, and Fortune Global 500s to small- and mid-sized family owned businesses, including such organizations as NASA, FRTIB, United States Army, Proctor & Gamble, AT&T, Schwan Food Company, Basin Street Properties, and Restoration Hardware. Judith is known for supporting teams in becoming more efficient and effective by developing people and relationship skills.

From 1981 until 2004, Judith worked closely with Will Schutz, Ph.D., the creator of FIRO theory. Considered one of the world's leading experts, Judith mentors facilitators, coaches, therapists, and other professionals in the integration of the FIRO theory in their work.

Judith's flagship programs, Authentic Leadership 1: Become Your Authentic Self, and Authentic Leadership 2: Navigating the Interpersonal Word Mindfully, have been running since 2005 and are attended by people from all walks of life.

Judith and her husband, Daniel Ellenberg, Ph.D., are the co-authors of *Lovers for Life: Creating Lasting Passion, Trust, and True Partnership* and co-authored a chapter in Mastering the Art of Success: Volume 8. They are currently writing a book on Mindful Conversations®